# Facebook Marketing

## *A Guide to Growing Your Brand with Facebook*

**Jacob Kirby**

# Table of Contents

# Introduction

What do businesses, social media influencers, and brands all have in common?

While that seems like a setup for a terrible joke, it is a question that needs to be asked because, at the end of the day, they all need one thing: marketing.

All of them need marketing in some way, shape, or form to increase their presence to aim at the target audience. Simply put, it is how they grow themselves. Businesses need more customers to become aware of them and buy what they sell; influencers search for more followers, and brands depend on both to thrive. There are many avenues of marketing out there, and there have always been. But how do you pick the right one that will lead to success?

There is one form of marketing that has been gaining ground over the last twenty years, and that is social media marketing. Social media platforms have provided many people and businesses with a wonderful opportunity to market their products or services more easily and fruitfully. On social media, people can build networks, share information, find products they want, and eventually, buy them. Brands not only use them to increase their sales but also to engage their audiences since social media can influence consumers' decisions. Despite the main objective of marketing being selling, social media has provided marketing professionals with a new insight: Providing engaging content is the best strategy to grow.

Besides, social media have integrated data-analytics tools that allow deeper understanding of audiences, which provides relevant information to take the next steps. Traditional marketing channels haven't disappeared, but social media have developed a funnel that concentrates all the actions on the same platform. Promotion, connection, interaction, informing, and conversion... all these actions take place on social media. Therefore, social media isn't only effective: It is also easy and low-cost. That is the main reason why all kinds of businesses, companies of all sizes, and entrepreneurs draw upon social media to grow.

Among all social media, Facebook is the largest social network in the world, with the greatest audience and the most active accounts. Although its original objective wasn't commerce, today, practically any company or person who wants to be in business must have a presence on Facebook.

Marketing on Facebook has benefits both for B2B and B2C marketers, with a low investment of time and money compared to other traditional marketing channels, as well as a higher return on investment. There are two main ways to market your brand or business on all social media platforms: paying to advertise and growing organically.

Paid advertising allows you to reach a certain number of people over a certain period of time within your requirements. The benefit of this is that you can reach thousands of users that are currently active without having to get them to follow you or find you first. The social media platform can 'bring the advert' to the potential customer rather than you having to bring them to the advert.

Growing organically means that you grow your page on the social media platform by increasing your followers and the number of people visiting your page over time. The benefit of this is that your conversion rate will typically be higher than with paid advertising.

Both alternatives have the advantage of increasing the traffic to your website and will eventually have a multiplicative effect across your sales channels. Facebook is the front door of your business, and you must learn how to make profitable and effective use of it. Whether you already have a Facebook Page or are still questioning if you should, in the following chapters you will find the reasons and the tools to make some room for your brand on this social media network.

# Chapter 1: Facebook to

# Market Your Brand

The key point of marketing is to meet consumers' needs with the goods or services you provide that can satisfy those needs. Incredible marketing is the kind that shows consumers they have needs they yet don't even know. Social media have become among the most effective tools for meeting consumers' needs and providing solutions, even when they weren't looking for them. That is the main difference between social media and traditional marketing: While the latter was obviously driving sales, social media makes the users feel they have control. It turns the process upside down.

On social media, users come into contact with all sorts of content that will influence their decisions and lead them to desire, need, and ultimately buy, without even noticing it. Through social media content, users shape their opinions, preferences, and needs, as a part of the global interaction that happens within those large, borderless communities they belong to. Social media have two main purposes for marketing: They reach great audiences to promote a product or service, and they encourage interaction. This helps to build communities but also allows brands to receive some feedback from audiences, which is another remarkable advantage over traditional marketing channels.

Among all social media, Facebook places first in the ranking of the world's most active platforms with 2.934 billion monthly active users according to a July 2022 report. With a world population of 7 billion people, more than 40% of them have an active account on Facebook. Is there any other way you could possibly reach such an audience through any traditional marketing method?

Here is another significant statistic you probably will want to keep in mind: 73% of the global advertising audience on social media belongs to Facebook. These numbers show that despite the emergence of many other social network platforms, Facebook remains dominant. In fact, many of the new social media have come to be part of the Facebook company, now named Meta.

Meta hasn't only been disruptive in communication and marketing, but it is now revolutionizing the whole content market with the metaverse and its countless applications which are mostly yet to be discovered. However, Facebook's most basic features are enough to boost your business to levels you haven't imagined.

## Facebook and Branding

Whatever you do or sell, you're almost certainly not the only one. At the same time, nobody else can offer exactly the same product or service as you do. The key to letting people know that and making them choose you among all your competitors is **branding**.

Branding implies building the name and image of any organization, professional profile, product, or service with a particular meaning that will shape the consumers' minds. It is called **brand identity** and it helps your customers recognize you, remember you, and prefer you among others because they understand what makes you different and special. Then, the marketing strategy must seek to establish brand positioning: whenever the customers have a particular need, your brand will be the first option that comes to their mind.

The main purpose of marketing, as well as branding as a core process, is to draw customers and other stakeholders' interest and then make them want to come back. It implies a deep knowledge of the target audience. Consumers' decisions are determined by many factors such as needs, quality, and incentives, but they eventually lean towards the option that connects with their deepest emotions. Therefore, what gives a company an advantage over the competitors is the ability to connect with the consumers' emotions. Customers will pick the brand that fits best with their own identity: in other words, the brand that makes them feel the happiest and most comfortable.

Of course, the product or service the company, organization, or individual delivers must be aligned with the brand identity they have created. There is no engagement from the audience if there is no correlation between what is being offered and what they ultimately receive.

It should be clear now that developing your brand identity and marketing strategy will depend on how well you know your target audience. Facebook, as it is a social network where users have a central role, is an excellent source of information about what the audience wants, how they feel, and what they expect. Social media provide the channels to obtain feedback from the audience, and the opportunity to see and hear them when they may not expect it.

Once you have gathered enough information about your audience or you have defined your **buyer *persona***—that ideal customer you want to attract and retain—you're ready to design and apply a content strategy to improve your brand's positioning. Now, you'll see the importance of having an aggressive content strategy to enhance your presence on social media.

Social media and social networks like Facebook are all based on **content marketing**. As said above, traditional marketing channels conveyed messages with the main purpose of making a sale, or **conversion**. On social media, that is rather different because consumers' behaviors have changed. People don't feel comfortable being convinced to buy things. They—we, rather—prefer to believe that our buying decisions are all our free will. Therefore, messages that have an overt intention to sell don't tend to do well. Quality content has the ability to influence the consumers' free will and make them desire the product or service you offer.

However, a good content strategy on social media demands relevant and meaningful content for the audience. It isn't purely about the amount (though that is also important); it is about the quality. That's why a content marketing strategy needs planning and performance measurement. You need to check what is valued by the audience and what is not, but we'll come back to this at a later stage. Let's now take a closer look at your content strategy.

The content you will use on social media, and particularly on Facebook, must provide some relevant information to your audience—for instance, a solution to any trouble they might have. First, you need to have a clear idea of who your buyer persona is, and then define the **customer journey**. This is another important concept to take into account when designing successful marketing strategies. There is a whole process from the moment the person begins to consider a product, then decides to make a purchase, and finally completes the sale. That process is called the customer journey, and you need to decide at which moment of that journey your brand is going to assist the customer to satisfy their demands. The type of content you produce depends directly on the arc of the customer journey you envision for the brand.

In general terms, content production is a creative process with the main objective of building engagement with the audience. The content might have three possible intentions:

- to inspire
- to teach
- to entertain

Inspiring content invites users to develop a sense of belonging. Its objective is to persuade them through emotional motivation to achieve certain goals or take certain actions. The users' loyalty bond is built through that emotional connection.

Educational content tries to teach either about the product or service the company provides or about any needs the audience might have. Engagement will come when the customers feel that the brand provides useful information, beyond what it is trying to sell.

Entertaining content is, without a doubt, what performs best on social media. When users peruse social media, they aren't deliberately looking for things to buy, but they are looking to be entertained!

The good news is that Facebook is a versatile social network where all this content can be produced and easily shared. This places Facebook as one of the best platforms to anchor and develop branding for any business, big or small.

# Draw Customers in With a Facebook Page

Facebook has two possible types of users that will market on the platform: companies/organizations and people with professional profiles who pursue goals beyond mere entertainment or social interaction. Personal profiles are reserved for interpersonal interactions: sharing photos, staying in touch with friends, showing your achievements, and receiving congratulatory greetings and love. But for business, this is not the best option.

Personal profiles have a lot of limitations that will prevent your brand from growing to its full potential. For example, you won't be able to have more than 5 thousand contacts. It might seem like a huge number, but it is nothing if put against the sum of all active users on Facebook (over 2 billion every month). For that reason alone, using a personal profile to market your brand or company isn't the best idea.

On another hand, further rules and algorithms won't let you post certain content, because Facebook intends to preserve the spirit of a social network. If you frequently break the rules, Facebook can even suspend your account without warning.

Nonetheless, Facebook has another type of page for marketers, called a fan page.

First of all, let's see what a fan page is and the constituent elements of a great one. It is a business profile that provides users with different marketing tools to implement their strategies, schedule content, manage paid advertisements, dig into data analysis, and coordinate call-to-action buttons—all with the goal of reaching and serving a larger audience.

Among the many reasons that could be listed, we can point out the following to make it clear why a fan Page on Facebook is a must for your marketing strategy:

- It allows you to reach the audiences you've targeted in the past but also expand your brand awareness to new demographics.

- You don't need to add people and wait to be accepted to convey your messages, so your scope exceeds your initial network of contacts.

- The published content can go viral, increasing traffic to other social networks and websites. Your message will reach a wider audience; even users who aren't your followers.

- It allows interactions that help to raise engagement with the audience and increase organic growth.

- Competitors' profiles are available there as well, full of information about their products/services and their own marketing strategies. It is also possible to find other stakeholders to form alliances with to expand the business network.

- It provides the tools needed to create and manage marketing campaigns.

- It is very intuitive, which saves time; not much upskilling is required to make efficient use of the platform. You don't need to have special competencies to be an active user, so it is accessible to anyone with basic computer literacy.

- Despite the emergence of other social media, Facebook remains the most popular among people of all ages, all over the world.

- Facebook offers a broad range of possible ways to post content in different formats, depending on the message, the purpose, and at which stage of the sales funnel your prospective customers are in.

- It allows easy and natural interaction with the audience to enhance and increase conversation between the consumers and the brand.

- As a social network with increasing competitors, Facebook keeps evolving to update the available features, so the company is always at the forefront of innovation.

Last but not least, a brand without a fan page appears less professional. Facebook has gained such widespread recognition that it is now indispensable for any brand to have a business profile. When a new consumer wants to know about a company, an organization, or a professional, Facebook is often the very first place they look to learn more. This is a sort of cover letter for your business. For many businesses, building this page will be among the first steps to cultivating social legitimacy and gaining relevance.

The next step after realizing the importance of Facebook for your marketing strategy is to create an attractive business profile: your fan page. The whole profile must be totally aligned with the brand identity. It is a two-way road: Your Facebook profile helps to create and consolidate your brand identity, and at the same time, your fan page has to reflect it. When any user, from your local audience or from abroad, visits your profile, it's best if they recognize your brand immediately.

Every fan page is linked to a personal profile. However, if there isn't an important name behind the company or the organization, it can be anyone. If you're running a personal business or what you need is a professional profile, your personal account can be useful to lead followers from one page to another.

There are different types of fan pages, and you should choose the one that best fits your activities or the market niche of your business. Remember that Facebook as a platform for brand-building isn't only for products or service providers. Marketing isn't only the way to increase sales but also to expand your professional activities, whatever they may be. Facebook knows this and that's the reason why you can choose among six options of fan pages:

- Local Business or Place
- Brand or Product
- Company, Organization, or Institution
- Entertainment
- Cause or Community
- Artist, Band, or Public Figure

The right way to decide the correct option for your fan Page depends less on how you see yourself or your business, but more on how your buyer persona is going to look for you. Besides, each type has special features related to their respective category. Here, more doesn't necessarily mean better: The category you pick must reflect what you do, even if there are other options with more available features.

Some important aspects to creating a successful fan page on Facebook are as follows:

- Profile and cover photos: These are the first thing users see as they visit your business profile. For companies and organizations, you should use the brand logo, so that users will automatically recognize you. You should also use a color palette that matches your brand identity. Then, the users will know with certainty that they're not on an impersonator's page. If you change your cover photo periodically, you will increase visibility among your audience, as doing so will automatically display a notification for your followers.

- Choose an easy-to-search name: This is not the right place to be too creative. The name of the company, the organization, or your professional name will work. This is how your potential customers will look for you. You're allowed to use a maximum of 50 characters.

- Fill out the "About" section with all the relevant information about your business. This is the place to speak about the mission, vision, and goals, but also to share useful information to lead the visitors to your storefront, be it digital or brick-and-mortar.

- Add a "call to action" button. One of the best features of social media is the ability to invite users to interact with your account. You can choose among options, like "Watch Video" or "Sign Up," and then customize these options.

Fan Pages provide a wide range of tools and resources to create successful marketing campaigns. Having a clear idea about the brand identity, the buyer persona you're wanting to attract, and a well-designed plan are key aspects to achieving success when marketing on Facebook.

# Chapter 2: Growing Strategies

# on Facebook

After setting up the appropriate profiles for your business, the next step is to plan a content strategy. Substantial and consistent growth requires much more than posting content periodically. All the content must have a purpose and be coherent with the brand's image.

The guidelines for selecting, producing, and programming the content to be posted depend on the target audience. Clear goals are important, such as: create community, increase sales, build awareness, or go viral, among others. The goal will help you to determine the type of content to produce and the best tools to produce it. Later, we shall cover various types of content that you may like to produce.

Facebook, like any other social media platform, works with algorithms—sets of calculations that decide what will appear on the users' screens or newsfeeds. These algorithms analyze data to make predictions about what the users want to see according to their previous research and visits on all social media. The conclusion is that, to lead your target audience to your profile, make them want to stay, and entice them to return, you need to produce content they value, save, and share.

## Organic Growth

Organic growth is related to organic reach. The organic reach of an account refers to all the unique users that visited or saw the profile on their feed or your page, as a result of unpaid posts. It includes the number of people that see a post from a profile through unpaid distribution.

Facebook's search engines provide results based on aspects like the frequency of the posts and the popularity determined by user interaction. Through analyzing posts, Facebook ranks the content based on how likely a user is to interact with it. So, in this way, Facebook has the power to place your content on the feeds of users who are most likely to engage with it.

In a nutshell, this means that organic reach targets mostly your base audience, genuine contacts, and followers who already know you, but the more often you post and the more interactions you get from them, the more likely your profile will reach other users organically from outside your particular network—all without paid distribution.

Three factors influence how an account performs in that ranking:

- Inventory: This refers to all the posts of friends, groups, and accounts followed by the user.

- Passive and active signals: The former are those that don't depend on users' actions, such as viewing or posting time; the latter are those coming from users' interactions.

- Predictions: Facebook anticipates what the user will choose to interact with according to previous behavior on the platform.

In 2022 there were changes to Facebook algorithms with the intention to limit the emergence of undesired content on users' feeds. Despite organic reach having your followers as the target audience, the objective beyond this is to generate interactions that will lead your content to outsiders and result in more followers. This way, your content will progressively rank better so that it will appear on the feed of users that don't follow you yet.

New algorithms add new restrictions to that flow of content. So, it is now more difficult to increase organic reach, but it is not impossible. One of the reasons that might affect organic reach, besides the new cues of the algorithm, is that there is more and more content being posted, so the competition is stronger. Besides, Facebook users have features to customize their experiences on the network and have personalized feeds. Therefore, to convey your message to those personalized profiles, you need to provide interesting and engaging content.

Even though Facebook provides the alternative of paid distribution, it is important to dedicate part of your marketing strategy to organic growth.

There are simple actions that can be implemented in your content strategy to boost organic reach:

- **Use more visual and audiovisual content.** This sort of content is more effective than text on Facebook. It makes users stay longer on your feed or post and encourages higher rates of interaction.

- **Schedule the posting.** There are moments of the day when users are more active on social networks. By learning when your audience is most likely to be online, you can be strategic and have Facebook publish your post at that time— increasing the potential for users to interact with it. This is a core element of any organic reach strategy.

- **Find a flow.** Periodical posting is one of the most important factors, but you don't want to overwhelm your audience. It is difficult to balance quantity and quality; you should prioritize the quality while also creating a good schedule posting. You may like to test posting different quantities for a few weeks to determine which number of posts per day/week results in optimal engagement. More isn't always better.

- **Follow trends and use hashtags.** Social media is about taking part in global conversations. Hashtags allude to what people are talking about. It is an easy way to learn the audience's interests. You should use trends to get involved in relevant conversations and add the personal touch that will make you stand out from the crowd.

- **Avoid clickbait.** Algorithms also control the quality of the published content. Excessive clickbait and posts with links drawing the audience away from your page typically don't perform well, especially not over the long-term.

- **Post quality content.** This is obviously easier to say than to do but it is the most effective way to engage your audience.

Facebook also has a feature that works to keep your audience updated and attentive to your posts. This feature is the ability to turn on notifications for your posts, so that your followers will be notified every time you post on Facebook. You can make a call-to-action post to ask followers to activate their notifications for your profile's posts. This is a great way to increase organic reach, so long as you're posting quality content your audience is happy to be notified about!

## Meaningful Interactions

To increase organic reach, the published content needs to be high quality and make your audience want to interact with it. These are called meaningful social interactions—MSI—and they hold special value in the algorithm.

Comments, likes, and shares are the most frequent meaningful interactions among users. This means that algorithms won't solely reward time spent scrolling on a profile's feed or watching a posted video. To rank higher on Facebook, your account needs to get your followers active by interacting: sharing the content on their own News Feed, tagging friends and family in the comments, or reacting to the posts.

To boost MSI within your profile, you need to create content that meets your target audience's interests and that makes them feel part of the global conversations that we have already covered. A way to increase MSI is by encouraging collaborative interaction among your followers. A great way to do that is by creating or becoming part of groups where people join according to their interests.

It has been pointed out that quality content is crucial. A way to generate MSI is by creating outside-the-box content. That is, innovative and disruptive content in different formats that will surprise the audience and make them want to share it. Following trends will place you in relevant conversations but this type of content will reveal what makes you different from and unrivaled by your competitors. Inspiration can come from other brands' campaigns, posts from your followers, and vintage ideas to be recycled. Try to think like your buyer persona and imagine what they would expect—or wouldn't expect— to see what kind of content you could produce.

Then, you must take advantage of the main benefit that social networks provide: the possibility to build large communities and get people to feel that the brand is the bond that ties them together. Plan a marketing strategy to position your brand somewhere your followers can belong. Your brand reflects a shared vision of the world. Building community implies promoting conversations between you and your audience, as well as between individual audience members. It is an outstanding and revolutionary feature of social networks for branding.

Meaningful interactions will make your profile's activity on Facebook turn into conversions. This doesn't exactly mean that the social network will become your main sales channel. Facebook has tools to funnel sales traffic, but the main purpose of the marketing strategy on Facebook is to increase branding, build a loyal bond with your audience, and make them identify with the values of the brand. Every time your content shows on their News Feed, they should ideally feel the brand deeply matches their own interests and wishes, even those they didn't know they had.

## Messenger: Stay in Touch with Your Audience!

A key point to building community through social media is having fluent interaction with your audience. People want to know about you and, as we've seen, you also need to know about your target audience. So, effectively using all the communication channels Facebook provides, will result in productive interaction with your audience because they will feel more involved and confident in the brand.

The chance to have direct and constant feedback from the audience is what turns the relationship between seller and buyer upside down. Traditional marketing channels had unilateral means of communication, and they would figuratively "shout" at the audience to make them buy things. Social networks have turned that communication into horizontal channels where the brand can talk to consumers, as well as listen to and learn about them. The purpose is to prove that the brand can understand their needs and be part of the solutions, but it is a more implicit message. The consumer is part of the conversation that will eventually lead them to choose the brand over others.

Facebook, like other social networks, provides a lot of ways to stay in touch with your audience. For instance, you can react every time a user shares your content. This is one way to express gratitude to the user and get to be seen twice on their notifications, improving your position in the ranking. If you comment on shared content, you will be opening a conversation not only with this follower but with their audience, which will also increase your visibility.

It is also recommended to answer all the comments on any post that has tagged your account. Even if it is a critic, it is very negative for the brand to ignore direct mentions from the audience. Besides, you'd be losing the opportunity to take part in conversations you didn't begin but were invited to. It is a good way to scope a wider audience and grow organic reach.

However, the top communication channel on Facebook that allows direct interaction with followers is Messenger. This chat app is embedded in the social network and connects all users, even if they do not follow your fan page, or for personal profiles if they are not part of your network of contacts. Messenger breaks down the barrier of impersonal connection between a brand and the audience through a screen, which used to be an obstacle to building trust and loyalty.

However, this creates a new obligation for the fan page user: You must always answer direct messages. If you neglect to check your Messenger inbox, it portrays the image of a brand that does not value their customers, and this casts a shadow over all the other marketing efforts you put forth. Put yourself in your followers' shoes: Would you still be interested in a profile that doesn't update its content? It doesn't matter if you have the best content schedule... Users search for personal interaction with the brand, and one place that is found is on Messenger. So, if you do not check or answer your messages, your audience will feel you are not interested in keeping their attention. That's not good for the business!

Hopefully, your Messenger inbox will receive a lot of messages; this situation demands expenditures of time and effort to read and respond to each one. Fortunately, Facebook considered this and provides a feature to prepare automatic answers that are conveyed when a user sends you a direct message. You can customize a greeting message to welcome a user that is reaching out to you for the first time. Facebook has preset answers, but you can modify the message to align with the tone of your brand.

You can also choose among different preset automatic questions that have answers by default. These answers are automatically sent when the user asks one of those questions. People are aware that those are preset answers, that they aren't being written in the moment by a representative of the brand, but still feel that you're helping to satisfy their demands. A kind message saying "Leave your question, someone will contact you soon" is more comforting than an empty white box.

There is another feature on Messenger that allows you to program certain answers when a message enters the inbox and the account is inactive. This way, regardless of when a user wishes to contact the brand, there will always be someone there to answer.

# Chapter 3: Deciding the

# Content of Your Posts

The content strategy is the core of the whole marketing strategy. There is no sense in planning an omnichannel campaign or investing lots of money either in the production of sophisticated content or paid advertisements if there isn't a connecting bond that gives meaning to all the posts. Each post is a decision, a part of a bigger message your brand needs to clearly transmit to the audience. Then, the sequence, the frequency, and the measurement of the posts' performances constitute the rest of the process.

The essential recommendation is to post regularly, but that doesn't mean that you should simply post anything that comes to mind just to keep your posting rhythm. You should create a content strategy that you can stick to over time; in this way, you'll earn a reputation for consistency. Posting on relevant days with specific significance for your audience is another way of building community and helps you find relevant content to create your posts. For instance, if your niche is technology, you probably won't post about World Elephant Day or Independence Day of a country that isn't your primary audience's.

There has to be a concept behind all the content to be published, with a meaning aligned with the brand's identity and according to the target audience characteristics. When it seems that there are no further ideas for innovative content, you can always turn to your audience. You can try to find out which type of content would motivate your audience, and you can use Facebook features to keep adding value to the community. One way to get started is asking them what they want to see. Sometimes, if the community doesn't get involved in conversations, you can start one. Any sort of post can help to open a conversation, discuss a new product, or find out frequent questions users might have about your product or service that isn't included on the fan Page.

Even when you're in charge of the marketing strategy and are the one who plans, creates, and distributes the content, it is always the audience that sets the pace.

## Facebook Posting Alternatives

In Chapter 1, we discussed how recognizing the buyer persona leads to a better conception of the target audience. In addition, figuring out the customer journey is an important step to deciding at which stage of this journey your brand is going to help your customer meet their needs and complete their purchase. There are specific formats for the different types of content you need to produce to meet your target audience's expectations and successfully accompany the customer through their journey. A message in the wrong format will have adverse outcomes even if it is relevant information or is emotionally resonant.

Facebook allows many types of posts: comments, status updates, expressions of feelings, photos, and videos, among others. All of these can work, sometimes in tandem, to build engagement with the audience if they are accurate and appropriate for the message you're trying to convey. However, there is evidence that audiovisual content is more engaging than any other form. Our brains process images more quickly than text, so people are more likely to pay attention and understand a message conveyed if it has visual support.

However, some posts with text can be effective call-to-action messages and compel your audience to interact. For instance, you can include questions with options to answer or react, use status updates to express feelings or emotions, or fill-in-the-blank tasks for people to complete something about your business. In general, there isn't a lot of text in this type of post and to make them more attractive, easy to read, and engaging, you can always use emoticons. They give the text a friendlier tone that readers can't help but react to.

To post visual content, Facebook has a lot of options: photographs, carousels, native videos, and live video streams. Any of these can be a good resource as long as it fits the brand's identity and the message it conveys matches the goals of the company, organization, or professional.

Photo-based posts are always key resources. All people love looking and sharing photos, but they can't be photos of just anything. They have to reflect the brand in some way. Even when they are more subtle, like a creative campaign that uses metaphors and subliminal messages, it doesn't make sense to post things your audience won't understand. Traditional advertising campaigns use this sort of content to strengthen their brand identity. They implicitly broadcast the values the brand holds, and the audience will recognize this common ground. It is a way to connect with the audience and make the brand easily recognizable. It works well for the objective of brand building, but its message is less direct.

Creating interesting and colorful photo galleries and adding photos to your timeline definitely makes your profile more attractive to your followers, especially new visitors. After reading the "About" section to learn more about the profile and the product or service, photos are the next source of relevant information when a user reaches a profile they're interested in.

A new visitor is less likely to scroll through the News Feed of the profile they're visiting for the first time, but an attractive photo gallery will catch their interest and lead them to learn some more. If there isn't any content, the profile might look abandoned. That visitor won't become a follower and there is little chance that they will come back.

Personal profiles can post any photo at any time, but in business profiles, there has to be a reason and a message.

Besides photographs, other graphic pieces can provide a versatile format to post all kinds of content: flyers and infographics, for example. There are several types of editing software and apps with thousands of preset templates that make it easier to create attractive content to provide information, for instance about the product or the service, to teach about something, or to create entertaining content. It is recommended to use trademark colors in all the posts so that followers will always associate the content with your brand. This helps to create continuity and lets the brand stick deep in users' minds.

Photos and graphic pieces can also be presented in a sequence. They are called carousels and they make the user stay longer on the profile. This is a useful format to present information, how-to guidelines, recommendations, and product/service descriptions, among many other types of information your users will be looking for. These kinds of posts tend to motivate more meaningful interactions. People can ask questions through the comments, tag friends or family to pass on useful information they have found, and can save the post to watch it again later. All this helps to increase organic reach, so it is worthwhile to dedicate time and creativity to this type of content.

There is a new type of content that has become massive in recent years and set many online trends, called 'memes'. According to the Merriam-Webster dictionary, a meme is "an amusing or interesting item (such as a captioned picture or video) or genre of items that is spread widely online, especially through social media". Trends are, in general, good marketing resources because everybody is talking about them; brands who use trending memes on their profiles have great chances to have their content replicated in other profiles and even outside the original social network. However, it's necessary to have a good strategy as a backup, and not to rely solely on trends for your marketing strategy.

The star format is, indeed, videos. Facebook has added a feature to display videos: Facebook Watch. This feature allows the posting of native videos or live transmissions, being a great option to reach the audience more directly. A key recommendation is that the videos shouldn't last more than two minutes, and the first nine seconds need to be irresistible for the user so that they will stay and watch until the end. While photos are still preferred to capture important moments, videos are chosen to connect more instantaneously with the audience, particularly live streaming to have virtual encounters in real time. It creates a new sense of proximity through the screen. It is the most valued resource for content creators and influencers, but anyone running a business can make a profit from video content, especially when it's skillfully edited and backed by a good content strategy.

Videos are the top engaging content and "watch video" is one of the most attractive call-to-action buttons to add to the fan Page on Facebook. However, live videos perform better on Facebook with more effective results on the algorithm.

Another useful resource that Facebook borrowed from other social networks is stories. They are attractive because of their short, concise, and entertaining content that is only available for 24 hours. Due to their ephemeral nature, users tend to check them constantly so that they won't miss anything. (This phenomenon, called "FOMO"—an acronym for *fear of missing out*—has been studied and written about extensively, and is a powerful motivating force.) The content posted on stories can be photos or videos that display an immersive experience as they fully occupy the screen of cell phones. They are less attractive on other devices, but cell phones are where the majority of people use social media apps.

Stories are great to create continuity for your audience: If you constantly post content on stories, the audience will see your brand more often. Also, they are good medium for interacting with followers, as they have call-to-action emoticons to react to the story and the option to send an instant message directly from the post.

The most frequent content for stories is important announcements, celebrations, and sales promotions. In general, the content for stories is spontaneous and its aim is mostly to amuse or generate interaction, more than providing relevant information.

A great content strategy uses all these formats and types of content in a well-distributed calendar to alternately inform, educate, and entertain with consistent posts. The more varied your content is, the more likely your followers will want to save them, see new posts, and share them with their own social networks. All posts must be consistent with the brand's identity and meet the target audience's interests.

Like any other social network, Facebook is constantly adding and improving features. It is important to keep your strategy updated with this; it will evolve due to whatever happens on social media and changes in prevailing attitudes or trends. Interesting, quality content is always innovative.

## *Storytelling*

Storytelling is a technique that has become more and more used in branding. Companies and organization use storytelling to enter their audiences' lives with stories that might reflect theirs or inspire them. As it has been said, people don't want to be persuaded to make a purchase; the idea of having someone trying to sell you something is annoying rather than desirable. Marketing now has to create the feeling that people freely decide to get involved with a brand, and that acquiring a product or service is something more personal than an exchange of goods and money. Storytelling provides an innovative way for brands to connect and create a more intimate bond with the audience.

The main objective is to create emotional bonds with the audience through stories. People will find that these stories might be similar to theirs, but also like to know that there's a story behind the brand that makes them empathize with it.

A well-told story can influence people's decisions more than any other advertising strategy because it talks to their emotions more than their intellectual nuances. The background for those decisions is beyond reason, so the connection with the brand is stronger and more genuine. Good stories invite consumers to take action and to interact with the content, which eventually leads to becoming a part of the brand's community.

Telling stories is an ancient human method for bonding and building confidence. However, it cannot be just any story. It has to be something relevant, personal, and authentic. The audience must believe that behind all the literary resources that can be used, there is something real and worth discovering.

To decide which story to tell and how it will be presented, you need a clear target audience: The age and cultural background of the intended audience is most relevant. Also, it must be decided in advance which emotion the story will touch: happiness, fear, hope, inspiration, courage, and so on. As with all content, stories need to be consistent with the brand's identity.

The perfect story presents a journey in which there is always transformation, improvement, and learning. As with any story, people need to find things to take away from it. This implies that the story must be engaging but simple, with familiar characters that people will easily remember.

Consumers' behaviors have evolved over time and now, the story behind the brand is even more important than the features of the product or the advantages of the service. In the same way, brands do not compete purely in quality and price but on how much people feel identified with them.

There are several resources to tell a story on Facebook. Using videos is probably the most common and effective, but it is not the only one. You don't need to tell the whole story in a single post, so you can make mix-up formats to provide the consumers with many pieces to recreate the story. You can use photographs, videos, live streaming, timelines; the only limit is your creativity.

# Chapter 4: Engagement Matters

Engagement is a core concept in measuring the performance of marketing strategies on social media. It alludes to the level of reliance or commitment consumers have towards the brand. It can be measured through the interactions that posted content can generate among the audience. The more people like, share, or comment on a post, the higher the *engagement* the post has.

On some occasions, engagement is achieved spontaneously, but if you are running a business, you need to make things happen. Therefore, if your fan page needs more engagement, you should develop a content strategy to make it grow. If the audience doesn't start a conversation, then you can motivate it through posts and campaigns.

Facebook has a lot of resources to tap into to increase engagement on your posts. A higher engagement not only helps your page reach more people, as the algorithm rewards interaction, but it also helps you to improve the community among your followers. Creating posts that encourage engagement means that you will have followers interacting with you, as well as one another in the comments!

## How to Create a Community

Social media users don't just use these platforms for entertainment or as unidirectional information channels. They are there to connect and interact, both with brands and businesses as well as with one another. Therefore, brands need to build spaces for the audience to have that stage to become a protagonist and participate actively.

So, besides creating quality content, you must work on building communities where people can interact amongst themselves. Facebook provides you with different features for building community: groups, events, and catalogs, the last of which is more focused on sales.

## *Groups*

Facebook groups are communities that any user can create in order to gather people based upon common interests. According to data, Facebook groups comprise around 400 million people over the world. Posting and taking part in conversations within groups can boost your organic reach. If you implement a strategy that motivates your followers to share your content with their groups of interest, that will mean more visibility for your fan page. Besides, there you have an excellent tool to improve segmentation for your campaigns: Every group will tell you what they are interested in.

Posting content on Facebook groups helps your fan page reach out to people who might be interested in your business, and groups also build a sense of reliability. People are more likely to make a decision based on the group's opinion. That is, some posts in the group will be more impactful than others.

Groups are a good way to increase organic reach, but they can also, as you will see later, help you find segments to target further with paid advertisements.

However, creating and taking part in a group requires effort and commitment to make it a useful tool. It is totally worth it since engagement achieved by building community has long-term effects.

Facebook groups demand organization and active participation. There are three types of groups on Facebook: Public, Private, and Secret. The appropriate type for Facebook most business pages is public groups, which can be found by any user on the social network without special requirements. Private groups will give you more control over the community, but they will also restrict your reach. Many businesses will charge for access to their private group, and if you are running a coaching type of business, this may be a viable option for you. Just keep in mind that a private group won't help you reach any new customers.

When creating a group, it is important to fill in all the relevant information. In the description, you must focus not only on your brand but also on the purposes of the group: what users will find in it, what they will take away, and what they can provide. There are also co-habitation rules that need to be explicitly communicated for users to know and accept before even joining the group.

Then, you have to pick five tags that will identify the group and help users find it. All those tags must be directly related to your business, and you should avoid metaphors or vague terms; for example, if you sell books, do not use a tag that simply says "growth." Also, try to use the five available tags; the more tags, the better (since they are connected to search engines).

It is also important to set the location. It doesn't matter if you do not have a physical store or provide material services; people like to know that there is something tangible—something real—behind the business. So, don't leave that space empty. Pick the city where you are or where the central offices are.

Like the customization of your fan page profile, the profile and cover photographs of the group are also important. Pick photos that are linked to the brand, with colors that match your image.

Groups on Facebook can have many administrators and moderators. The administrator, or admin for short, is the only one who can assign different roles inside the group. Moderators have the huge responsibility of maintaining the flow of conversation, receiving and welcoming new members, intervening when any conflict arises, and managing new members. As the main purpose of groups is to create community, they also encourage collaborative interaction.

To keep the interest of the members and encourage participation, it is very important to maintain a tone aligned with the brand, be attentive to comments and questions, always provide answers, and highlight prominent contributions from the members. The goal is for your users to develop a true sense of belonging in the group.

## *Conversations*

Social networks were invented to promote conversations. This is the most remarkable advantage over traditional marketing channels, so you should use your Facebook fan page to create an active community that regularly engages in conversations. Facebook is still one of the most popular because it offers more options to interact and be part of conversations. It is the social network where people comment the most and get involved in all kinds of conversations—not only on personal profiles, but especially on business profiles. They are very likely to express opinions, ask questions, and answer other users' ones, all of which can be useful for your organic reach if you learn how to optimize it.

It can be controversial sometimes, but there are elegant ways to avoid difficult issues and lead the conversation to a more fruitful territory where you can talk about your brand and all the benefits of being a member of your community. Brands who dare to take part in every sort of conversation, even tough ones, are seen as more real and reliable. So, this helps to increase visibility as well as engagement.

## *Events*

Virtual environments have provided the opportunity to gather without sharing the same physical space. For business, this has become a great advantage. You can create an event to talk to your audience, teach them about a product or service, or encourage interaction, all online.

Some online events are online conferences—live streaming or videos—webinars, meets, workshops, presentations, celebrations, just to name a few.

Events are an incredible tool to increase organic reach, since you can invite people to your events outside your community of followers, and people can share them on their own profiles, further increasing reach.

This event feature allows you to set a place and date (down to the hour) for in-person or online gatherings. They don't need to be huge occasions. You can create an event to coordinate a live contest with prizes, launch a new product, or have a live interaction with your audience. The main objective is to call your audience's attention and give them the chance to participate.

Events can also be private or public. Each of these options has advantages that you can benefit from. While public events allow any user to have access and will result in a larger reach, private events enhance engagement as they benefit members of your brand's community, giving users a good reason to be a part of it.

## *Facebook Catalogs*

Facebook also has specific places to funnel purchases. Facebook catalogs are features that help you to promote your products and services and provide relevant information about them to consumers. It is like any traditional catalog. It has all products organized in categories with full descriptions that will help users to find what they want and learn all they need to know to make a decision, and finally, buy it. Catalogs are more effective when they have accurate photographs to show the product with as many details as possible. Those with photos are always more engaging than those with text alone.

It is important to include all the information a customer might need about the product or the service. Prizes are part of that information. Even if you think that your competitors will have access to sensitive information about your business, customers are more likely to purchase if they have all the required information when making a buying decision.

These catalogs, as they are online, can be customized to make them interactive and dynamic. They have many features and benefits, such as the following:

- You can link the catalog to other social networks and other sales funnels.

- Products and services can be organized into categories which will help users to find them more easily, and at the same time will show them similar or related products when they are navigating the catalog. The products from the catalog can be used in posts and stories, and tags can lead users to the category they look for.

- Catalogs are also effective to show available products on the web store. They can also have a strong impact on the users' experience. Users need to know if they will be able to buy what they are seeing. That is also a good reason to always keep your catalog updated.

- The Facebook catalog allows you to create collections. This way, users have access to all similar or associated products, presented in creative and visually attractive ways.

According to the market within which you run your business, you can choose from four types of catalogs:

- For E-commerce.

- Trips: flights, accommodation, transfers, tourist tours, and more.

- Real estate: for rent or sale.

- Vehicles: cars, trucks, vans, and more.

You must choose the catalog that best fits your business or activity to have access to the most suitable template to display your product or services.

Catalogs need to have relevant, reliable, full, and updated information. If a user enters a catalog and one of these aspects is missing, it can have an adverse impact on the user's experience. The user experience determines if they will trust the page enough to make a purchase, follow the page, and recommend it to others.

As with every feature on Facebook, there are certain specific rules about what can be included or not in a catalog and how to display descriptions. It is important to meet all those rules to avoid issues or even a suspension of your account.

# Chapter 5: Facebook Ads: How to Create

# Successful Campaigns

Besides organic growth and its effectiveness, Facebook has specific tools for businesses to help you improve your performance on social media and increase your sales. Facebook remains the best and most effective channel for marketers to run paid campaigns.

As Facebook has cared about users' satisfaction, giving them all the control to customize their experience and have on their News Feeds only the content they choose to see, the network has also improved the options to make successful paid campaigns.

## Paid Content

Organic reach isn't the only way to expand your audience and increase conversions. Paid content campaigns can increase the interactions, traffic led to the website, conversions, and number of followers to make your community grow.

In general terms, brands look to make loyal bonds with their audiences, and most of the efforts are directed to enhance that link, making consumers choose the brand because they identify with its values. However, what any business needs ultimately is to grow. A business needs to sell products or services and to achieve that, it needs not only to have loyal customers, but to continually acquire new ones. This implies spreading outside their community of followers, who have already built that bond with the brand, and reaching all those who don't know anything about them, or don't know enough to prefer them over the competitors.

Organic reach can bring new visitors to your fan page, but paid advertisements can have far stronger effects in shorter periods of time.

## *Facebook Ads*

Facebook Ads is one of the best tools to make your business grow. It allows you to create sponsored posts in a wide range of types: text, videos, carousels, photos, or a mix of them, that pursue the objective of reaching out to an audience beyond your community of followers. The main advantage of Facebook Ads is that it provides the means to target broad audiences and identify great possibilities for segmentation. This means that you can customize your advertisement according to specific characteristics of your audience considering age, location, and interest, among other factors.

Advertising on Facebook doesn't have increased sales as the only objective. All types of businesses and activities have good reasons to advertise on Facebook. It is an amazing tool for e-commerce and to develop local businesses, as you can promote your products or services using a wide scope platform, with the possibility of targeting a specific audience to lead either to your online store or physical interaction.

However, advertising on Facebook is useful for organizations or institutions that provide other kinds of services, like education, information, or community activities. Promoting their services and activities through Facebook Ads helps to raise their social reputation, and get more people involved in their projects.

To create successful campaigns in Facebook Ads, it is very important to understand the algorithm. Algorithms will always tell which type of content the audience wants to have on their screen: If you launch a paid campaign with undesired content, the advertisement will reach the audience, but it won't have positive effects. If it is content irrelevant to the users, the paid advertisement won't promote interaction or make them want to follow your fan page.

So, after deciding what content you think will work best for your target audience, you need to decide the specific objective for the campaign. You can decide among three types of objectives:

- Recognition. This objective intends to increase interest from Facebook users in the product or service you have to offer.

- Consideration. This refers to the intention to increase interest in your company from users that get to see your paid advertisement.

- Conversions. This objective refers to increasing your sales through paid advertisement.

The most effective objective pursued by Facebook Ads is consideration. It consists of obtaining more interactions from the audience with the content, and more traffic from the fan page to the website or online store. Traffic campaigns are more likely to turn into conversions, but interactions are the best to improve branding.

According to the objectives you determine, you can choose among the following different types of formats: posts, text ads, videos, events, retargeting, and image ads. The most appropriate format will depend on the type of content you're posting. If your main target is to increase conversions, you need to know all about the decision processes users follow before buying, such as how they search for information, which competitors they also search before making a choice, and how many times they check products or services before completing the process.

Facebook Ads have many advantages. The most important is that you can decide the budget for your advertisement as you can decide how much you want to spend, select how many days you want your post to be promoted, and how large the audience you intend to reach will be. It is very flexible so you can optimize the performance of your advertisement. You can also customize the strategy and decide if you want to gain impressions and clicks, expand your reach, or direct more visitors to your website.

Another interesting feature that makes Facebook ads a great option to grow your business is that you can add very effective call-to-action buttons. If you have created engaging content, it will be easy for the user to take actions like booking, contacting, getting access, downloading, and much more. Even if the user does not choose to follow your page, the outcome is still positive since you're getting meaningful interactions.

Now, let's consider the most relevant components that a Facebook ad needs to have to be successful. As said above, visual content always performs better, but is highly recommended to accompany images and sounds with strategical copywriting to enhance the message conveyed. Here are some tips to create a good post for ads:

**Create engaging titles:** The first line of a post is the next thing the user sees after their attention is captured by the photo or video. Like the first three seconds of a video, the first line of the copy must make the user want to continue until the end. The use of emoticons can be visual support for the text.

**Write interesting text:** Even if the video is clear or the photo is self-explanatory, the text will help the audience better understand the message you want to communicate. You can add questions and surveys and use emoticons and hashtags. All the elements you include must be consistent with the overall concept of the post. Making a text more visual shouldn't lead you to use resources that distort the message. Humor isn't always the best option; informality isn't consistent with every brand identity. Go with what suits your brand's identity.

**Include graphic pieces:** Here you can choose from photos, flyers, infographics, single posts, or a carousel. The type of format depends on the content. Try to think how the user will best receive the message. If you have chosen storytelling, a sequence of images would be a good choice; if you're promoting a Black Friday sale, one single effective slide will work better. In any case, the quality of design, inclusion of high-definition photographs or videos, and the use of trademark colors are always recommended. The user might be seeing your brand for the first time, and you want them to remember it.

**Add call-to-action buttons:** You can add a call-to-action in the text, but Facebook ads also allows you to add buttons to the post. For instance, you can invite the user to visit your profile, "like" your fan Page, and send you a message. This is the best way to obtain more meaningful interactions and will get you to perform better on Facebook's ranking.

Another tool to make the most profit from Facebook ads is **Facebook Pixel**. This feature is a code that helps you optimize the performance of paid posts by measuring and gaining information from your visitors' profiles. Therefore, you can learn what type of content they prefer and use it to design your campaign. Pixel allows you to create a customer journey to learn what makes visitors buy, share, and like, and if they bring in the expected audience, you can retarget the campaign to attract them.

## *Some Recommendations*

Despite the temptation when creating paid advertisements to reach as many people as your budget allows you, it is always advisable to instead target a segment of your audience. If you talk to the wrong people, you will be negatively affected in two ways: it will worsen your performance on Facebook ranking and you will waste time and money.

Customizing the audience according to geographical location, age, gender, profession, and interests will ensure that your money brings about the expected outcomes. The main intention shouldn't only be to get more clicks or increase followers, but also to increase interaction. This is an objective with long-term results, as in the end, it will result in more organic growth.

Finally, organic growth is useful and provides limitless options if you have creativity and a great content strategy. However, Facebook Ads Manager is the most efficient tool to make your business grow quickly, and there is no reason to avoid it. Running a business always implies investing money, in particular, in marketing campaigns. Among all the possible means to implement a marketing strategy, Facebook is the one that combines low cost, easy implementation, constant measurement and evaluation of performance, and faster results.

# Chapter 6: Metrics & KPIs

Any strategy in business needs above all to be designed according to previous research to know the target audience and certain preset goals to achieve. Then, it requires a sequence of steps to implement the strategy. In this case, a marketing strategy on Facebook needs careful planning of unpaid and paid distribution posts to increase all types of reach simultaneously. The next stage is to measure and evaluate the performance of the published content to decide if the strategy is leading to the expected results or if they are not being accomplished as predicted.

Measurement and evaluation of the strategy don't need to be placed at the end of the process. In fact, it is an iterative process: Measurement and analysis of performance along the whole campaign allows you to make the necessary changes when things don't work as expected.

It might be difficult to decide what and how to measure. Sometimes, personal insights might lead to mistaken conclusions. You might be very happy with a campaign because the photos were amazing, and the story you told was very touching, but the bottom line is that if your audience didn't have a responsive reaction, it was ineffective. That is why social media, and for this matter, Facebook specifically, provides you with the accurate tools to have significant statistics to determine if your campaign is having the expected outcomes.

Facebook Insights provides you with all sorts of statistics to help evaluate your posts' performance, so you can make necessary changes in future campaigns to further optimize your campaigns.

# What are They and Why do They Matter?

The first thing to take into account is that not all statistics are relevant to your strategy. Almost every aspect of reality can be measured somehow, and on social media, there are a lot of metrics that you can use. However, dealing with big amounts of information won't guarantee a better understanding of what changes to make. Instead, it will be more of a waste of time or even lead you to incorrect assumptions.

While every KPI is a metric, not every metric is a KPI. Here there is a significant difference to understand Facebook Insights. Metrics are any type of quantifiable information that can be measured. That is anything that can be counted and expressed through numbers, percentages, and rates.

To track particular aspects of the business or the running strategy, for instance, you need the right indicators. These are KPIs: Key Performance Indicators. They are linked to the core target of the business. It means that each business, each marketing effort, and content strategy will have different KPIs according to the preset goals.

Let's see an example: if the objective of your strategy was to expand your social network on Facebook, KPIs won't be the same if you were trying to traffic your audience to your website, or if the final objective was to convert visitors into purchases. Each of them needs to measure different types of user behavior.

Nonetheless, it is equally important to track both metrics and KPIs, just with a clear idea of what destination all that information will take you to. While metrics will provide an overall evaluation of the business and allow you to identify pain points in your users' experiences when they interact with your brand through Facebook, KPIs will spot specific aspects of the strategy to reinforce or adjust.

## *Facebook Insights and Facebook Audience*

## *Insights*

Facebook has two tools that allow you to track metrics and KPIs, which are Facebook Insights, and Facebook Audience Insight. Facebook puts these two easy-to-use resources at your fingertips to provide a constant stream of relevant information. Once you learn to read the statistics and graphics, it becomes a natural stage of strategy implementation.

Facebook Insights is an analytics dashboard where you can track user behavior and post-performance on your Facebook business page. In addition to providing key metrics like page views and post reach for paid and organic posts, the platform also recommends competitor pages to watch and track. They allow us to track audience engagement metrics as well as factors like demographical information about the audience, how they behave and interact with the content, their engagement with the fan page, and also some information about competitors.

The "Insights" button is found in the sidebar of the home page of the fan page. There, you'll have the access to different charts with data about actions on the page, views and previews, likes, posts, and stories reach, among others. There is also a chart with specific information about the performance of your posts: how many profiles each of them reached, among other measurements of their engagement. To help you dive into metrics, Facebook has classified the information into categories such as followers, ads, reach, page views, and actions.

This is key information to better understand your audience, identify what kind of content gets more engagement, and make all necessary changes to the overall strategy, or some little adjustments to the posting calendar to reinforce or replace a certain type of content.

The other tool, Facebook Audience Insight, is used for ad campaigns and helps marketers understand Facebook audiences in general (which can also include those who follow your page). These are also referred to as 'Ads Insights API'.

## *What and When to Measure*

To have a deep understanding of what is relevant to measure on Facebook and make an accurate analysis of data, there are two main concepts to take into account: reach and impressions.

- **Reach:** This shows the number of people who've seen content published on the fan page. This category is split into types: tracking organic and paid traffic, respectively.

- **Impressions:** This is the number of times a post published on the fan page was shown on users' screens. Organic impressions count the number of times users viewed your post published for free; paid impressions refer to those users' screens where your post reached through ads distribution.

The first metric is more general and approximate while the second is more specific and precise.

Let's now take a closer look at all the actions on the page and audience interactions that can be measured on Facebook:

**Page views:** This is the number of times the page is reached within Facebook or from outside the social network.

**Page likes or follower growth:** This is the number of Facebook users that have clicked the "Like" button and therefore, are now fan page followers. You should not only measure how many followers you gain but also how many you've lost.

**Actions on page:** These metrics count the number of actions any user takes on the fan page, for instance, clicking on a website link.

**CTR (Click-through Rate):** This is calculated by dividing the number of link clicks by the number of impressions. In a nutshell, it counts the number of clicks on a post. Facebook still has the highest rate of CTR among all social media networks. It is applied both to free and paid posts.

**CPC (Cost per Click):** This specifically measures paid advertisements. It calculates how much money was invested in each click the paid post received.

**Post reach:** This refers to the number of Facebook profiles that have accessed your post.

**Post engagement:** It counts the interactions users had with the post: reactions, likes, shares, and comments.

**Best time to post:** As discussed earlier, the importance of planning includes knowing when it is the best moment of the day and the week to post content. This is related to moments of the day when audiences become more active. According to published data, on Fridays, there are 17% more comments, 16% more likes, and 16% more shares. During the week, the best time to post is between 1-4 PM. However, these are generalized statistics, and depending on your business you might get better results at different times of day/week. This is why it's important to track and test different strategies for increasing engagement.

Then, there are some specific metrics to measure the performance of videos:

**Minutes viewed:** This is the total amount of minutes that users stayed watching a video posted on the page.

**Video views:** Videos are displayed automatically as the users reach them while they're scrolling. To make it count as a video view, the user must watch the video for three seconds or more.

**Audience retention:** This is included in video metrics as it shows how long a user watches a video posted on your page.

At first, this may seem like too much information to process. However, metrics are crucial to measuring your fan page performance and engagement with the audience. Each of them shows a particular aspect of the page and the behavior of followers interacting with it. The KPIs that will be selected are defined by the specific objectives you choose when planning the strategy.

## *Reporting Facebook Insights*

All these metrics generate a considerable amount of information that needs to be systematized and later, analyzed. If you do not have an accurate register of these data, you won't be able to make useful changes as a result.

Therefore, the way you utilize Facebook Insights is crucial to have a correct understanding of your metrics. The main purpose of a report of metrics and KPIs is to reflect the performance of a campaign or the brand, depending on the period of time or the indicators that have been chosen. They show the impact of the implemented strategy and allow the evaluation of results according to the preset goals.

There are many benefits to making reports of Facebook metrics:

- It is the best way to keep track of all the results of a campaign on Facebook, contrast it with others, and ponder results within an overall strategy.

- A clear and organized presentation of statistical data is the best way to track effectivity without any subjective distortion.

- Accurate and timely information can prevent you from making the wrong decision or basing them on mistaken assumptions.

- It is the most reliable way to know the return on investment (ROI) of the whole strategy.

This is not solely for companies that have a community management team or a communication department. Any business or professional activity that has a marketing strategy needs to follow some steps to make it succeed. Knowing how it performs and measuring results are among the most important of those steps.

Facebook Insights and API provide updated statistical data every day. However, numbers are useful information only when they are accurately used. It isn't advisable to check insights every day or just after a new campaign is launched or a post is published to stay aware of how it's performing.

Facebook Insights and API data need to be dumped into appropriate templates. The way these data are presented affects how well the information is understood. There isn't any preset foolproof template, so each marketing manager will decide which works better for their specific needs. APIs, on another hand, have a feature to export the information in a preset file.

It is also important to decide which content is relevant and deserves to be included in the report, and which can be left aside. As said previously, more isn't always better. In the same way, the right amount of information is more useful when it is well-systematized and presented. The final report should highlight only the main data and it must be clear if the objectives were or were not achieved.

## *Facebook Insights: Keys to Interpreting Data*

Numbers and statistics can be tricky, particularly if you aren't a specialist. The most important thing is to know which questions you need to answer in regard to the performance of the business. That will help narrow the indicators you have to measure and track.

These questions can easily come from the objectives you set for the initial strategy. The more constrained those objectives are, the better to measure performance.

# Conclusion

In the global market, everybody needs to satisfy demand, and offer a solution of some kind. It is just a matter of being in the right place and communicating accurately. Long ago, market studies had to spend lots of time and money to conclude which business would be most profitable to run, where to sell products or services, and how to reach the right consumers. Marketing is the art of persuading people to consume, either those with intent, or those who've found it due to marketing campaigns.

Just a few years ago, some rules started changing. Now, marketing strategies are based mostly on social media. Consumers' behaviors have changed, therefore the way to reach them has to adapt to those changes. While in the past, marketing campaigns tried to install products in the market to increase the company's sales, now the relationship has turned upside down. The marketing mission is to learn what people are interested in, what their needs are, and how they would prefer to satisfy them. Then, companies will make an effort to speak to them in a way the audience will listen.

Social media have created larger, borderless communities where people from anywhere can get involved in global conversations that will shape trends and consumption habits. This internet-based social networking has become fruitful territory for companies to grow their marketing strategies. There, companies, organizations, influencers, and professionals, can reach out to make their products and services meet people's needs. Through social media, companies don't intend to persuade people to buy, but rather, show how much they have in common, and how brands can make them happier, and feel more satisfied.

Companies don't sell people products; people choose brands that reflect their own identities.

Among all social media networks, Facebook still remains the most popular with the most active users all over the world. Despite the many competitors that have arisen in the last few years, Facebook always finds a way to update its features and keep adding tools to make it a powerful marketing resource for all kinds of business and nonprofit activities.

I hope you have found this book to be informative and insightful with regard to marketing on Facebook. The social media landscape is constantly changing and evolving, with new features, algorithms, and trends emerging on a seemingly constant basis. The next step is to set up a Facebook page for your brand or business and begin implementing some of the strategies shared within this book!

Thanks for taking the time to read this guide, and I wish you the best of luck in your endeavors marketing on social media!

# References

Bretous, M. (2021, April 14). *A Beginner's Guide to Facebook Insights [+ Step-by-Step Instructions]*. HubSpot Blog. Retrieved September 15, 2022, from https://blog.hubspot.com/marketing/facebook-insights

Burducel, L. (2022, July 19). *Top 11 Most Important Facebook Metrics*. Socialinsider. Retrieved September 15, 2022, from https://www.socialinsider.io/blog/facebook-metrics/

Datareportal. (2022). *Facebook statistics and trends*. datareportal.com. https://datareportal.com/essential-facebook-stats

Stamper, J. (n.d.). *Meme Definition & Meaning*. Merriam-Webster. Retrieved September 15, 2022, from https://www.merriam-webster.com/dictionary/meme

Printed in Great Britain
by Amazon

23297251R00036